DR FRANCESCA FOTHERINGHAM

WONDERS of the MIND

UNDERSTANDING THE UNIVERSE INSIDE OUR HEAD

ILLUSTRATED BY **JAN BIELECKI**

WITH FOREWORD BY **PROFESSOR ANDREW TOLMIE OF THE BRITISH PSYCHOLOGICAL SOCIETY**

WAYLAND

the british psychological society
promoting excellence in psychology

To the generous and kind-hearted Kirsty Ross. – F.F.

To the unique minds in my life – J.B.

First published in Great Britain in 2024 by Wayland
Text © Francesca Fotheringham 2024
Illustration © Jan Bielecki 2024

Commissioning Editor: Grace Glendinning
Design: Peter Scoulding
Sensitivity consultation: Nicky Watkinson

Produced in association with the British Psychological Society, with thanks to:
Simon Goodson, Arden University, UK

ISBN: 978 1 5263 2534 1 HBK
ISBN: 978 1 5263 2536 5 PBK
ISBN: 978 1 5263 2535 8 EBOOK

Printed and bound in China

Wayland, an imprint of
Hachette Children's Group
Part of Hodder & Stoughton

Carmelite House
50 Victoria Embankment
London EC4Y 0DZ

An Hachette UK Company
www.hachette.co.uk
www.hachettechildrens.co.uk

WARNING: This book includes some discussion of mental health conditions. Please speak with a trusted adult if you think you may be experiencing one or more of them. Parents, teachers, carers or other trusted adults in your life may be able to help you understand what you are feeling, and connect you to the right place for dealing with your situation if needed.

There are also further resources on the last page of this book if you need to get help quickly, via phone or online.

The content in this book is for general information only and any medical advice should be sought from a doctor or other healthcare professional.

CONTENTS

4   WHAT IS THE MIND?

HOW IT WORKS

6   AN OVERVIEW OF THE BRAIN

8   THE BRAIN'S MANY PARTS

10 HOW THE BRAIN MAKES THE MIND THINK

12 CHEMICAL MESSAGES

14 OTHER ANIMALS AND THE MIND

16 THE CHANGING BRAIN

18 THE CHANGING MIND

20 EMOTIONS IN THE BRAIN

22 EMOTIONS IN THE MIND

24 HOW DOES REMEMBERING WORK?

26 TYPES OF LONG-TERM MEMORY

28 WHY DO WE SLEEP?

OUR MANY MINDS

30 MANY MARVELLOUS MINDS

32 EXPLORING THE WORLD OF NEURODIVERSITY

34 CAN HUMANS READ MINDS?

36 WHAT IS MENTAL HEALTH?

38 KEEPING OUR MINDS HEALTHY

40 CULTURAL PERSPECTIVES

42 HOW DOES LANGUAGE AFFECT OUR MIND?

THE AMAZING MIND

44 CELEBRATING THE HUMAN MIND

46 MIND GAMES

47 GLOSSARY

48 INDEX AND FURTHER INFORMATION

FOREWORD

This book is about understanding how the brain works and how it relates to our minds – which has been shown by psychologists to be key to healthy mental growth. Knowledge of the mind and its wonders helps us make sense of how we experience and think about the world and the people around us – rather than our thoughts, feelings or experiences being mysterious, confusing and even worrying. Realising where specific thoughts and feelings come from and what influences them helps us to manage them in a positive way.

Particularly important is the recognition that feelings, ways of thinking and our ability to learn are not fixed and that it is possible to change these. Recognising that it is possible to change our thoughts and feelings also helps us to become aware of the diversity in how *others* think and feel, and how this diversity arises from differences in our individual and shared experiences of the world – breaking down simple and prejudiced ideas about others.

Most important of all, we know that beginning to build this understanding of the brain and the mind at an earlier age rather than later helps children develop the abilities to cope with the stresses of daily life and to form secure relationships. By establishing these in childhood, they then become capabilities that can be extended when young people experience the challenges of adolescence – rather than those challenges becoming the source of later difficulties, as is currently the case for so many.

This is a fun book that I'm sure you will enjoy reading, but along the way, it will also help grow all this crucial understanding – a fantastic achievement!

Andy Tolmie

Chair of the British Psychological Society Research Board
Professor of Psychology and Human Development
UCL Institute of Education, London, UK

WHAT IS THE MIND?

We know we have this organ inside the skull called the brain, but what exactly is the *mind*? Is it in our brain? Is it in our heart? Or is it what some people call the soul?

The mind is very closely related to the brain. If the brain is the organ that makes our bodies do stuff, our mind is best described as our consciousness, which makes up our thoughts, feelings and who we are as a person.

Understanding 'consciousness'

Often you hear consciousness used to describe whether someone is awake or not, but it means a lot more than this.

Consciousness is all those things that let us know we're alive. Consciousness, or being conscious, means that you are aware of your thoughts, feelings, beliefs, memories and things that are happening around you. It also allows us to have an imagination and to pretend.

Scientists, philosophers, doctors and many other humans throughout time have been fascinated by this awareness and what it means.

Some scientists who study the **brain** are called **neuroscientists** (*neuro* meaning all things to do with the brain).

Scientists who study the **mind** are called **psychologists** (*psyche* meaning the mind and soul).

Researchers who study **why the mind exists** and **what it means to be a human** are often called **philosophers** (this comes from the Greek word *philosophia* meaning 'love of wisdom').

What makes us, *us*?

Every second of every day we experience life. This can be exciting things – such as playing with friends or going on holiday – but our life is also made up of all the little in-between moments when we feel like we're doing 'nothing' – such as waiting for the bus, brushing our teeth or sleeping.

All of these moments create our thoughts, feelings and experiences. All of these are completely unique to us and no two people in the whole world experience life in exactly the same way.

Changing brains, changing minds

In each of these split-second moments, our brain changes. It then uses these changes to help us know what to do in the *next* split-second moment. Over time, this creates our memories, beliefs and imagination – our minds.

AN OVERVIEW OF THE BRAIN

The brain is an organ that sits inside the skull, which is inside your head. This organ may look like a weird, squishy maze, but it does some pretty incredible things that allows us to think, feel and read this book.

Diagram of the outer brain

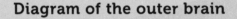

CEREBRUM
This is the name for the large, squiggly bit most people think of when they think about the brain.

The outermost layer of the cerebrum, with all the wrinkles on it, is called the CEREBRAL CORTEX.

CEREBELLUM
This bulgy bit at the bottom of the brain is called the cerebellum, which means 'little brain' in Latin. It helps us balance, coordinate and do a lot of the things we don't really think about doing.

BRAIN STEM
This connects the brain to the rest of the body and helps with some of our main functions to stay alive, such as breathing, digestion and body temperature. It is made up of the pons and the medulla (see page 8).

Zoom in on the cerebrum

FRONTAL LOBE
This lobe has many areas. For example, it has an area that helps us think (prefrontal cortex, see below), an area that helps us move (motor cortex) and an area that helps us put thoughts into words (Brocca's area).

PARIETAL LOBE
This is where our brain processes a lot of our senses. This includes taste, touch, pain, heat, sight, hearing and smell.

It also helps us know where our limbs are.

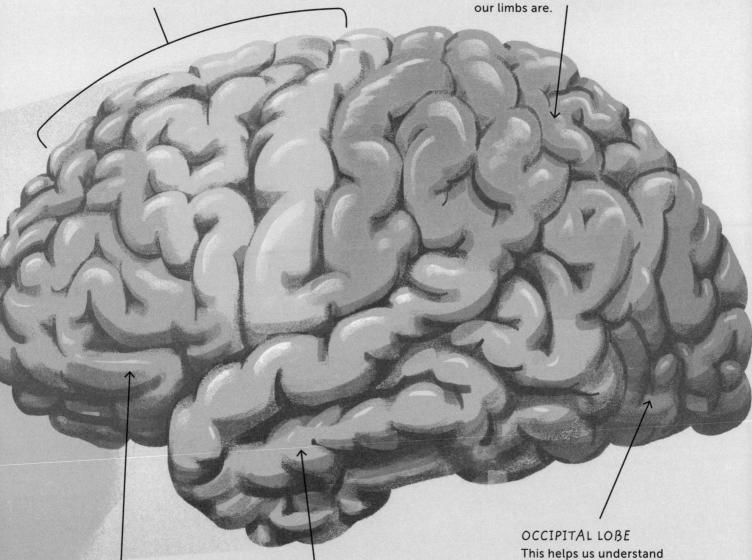

PRE-FRONTAL CORTEX
This part of the frontal lobe helps us do some of our most complex thinking, such as planning for the future, problem-solving and controlling our impulses.

It also helps us think through how to wait for something we want *now*, to get something better *in the future* (called delayed gratification).

TEMPORAL LOBE
This helps us with speaking. For example, remembering a word when someone says it to us, when we want to say it or when we read it on a page.

It also helps us recognise people and things, and can help us form memories.

OCCIPITAL LOBE
This helps us understand what we see, for example how far away something is, what colour it is, how big or small it is, or how fast it's moving.

It also helps us with making memories and recognising our friends' faces.

*W*hen our brain is in our skull, it's made up of 75% water, but when it's taken out and dried, 60% of our brain is fat!

THE BRAIN'S MANY PARTS

Let's have a look at your brain from a few different angles to discover some of the parts tucked inside.

Cross-section of the brain

You can get a good view of the many, complex parts of the brain by looking at different cross-sections. That means using diagrams that show what it would look like if you cut through the brain, top to bottom or left to right.

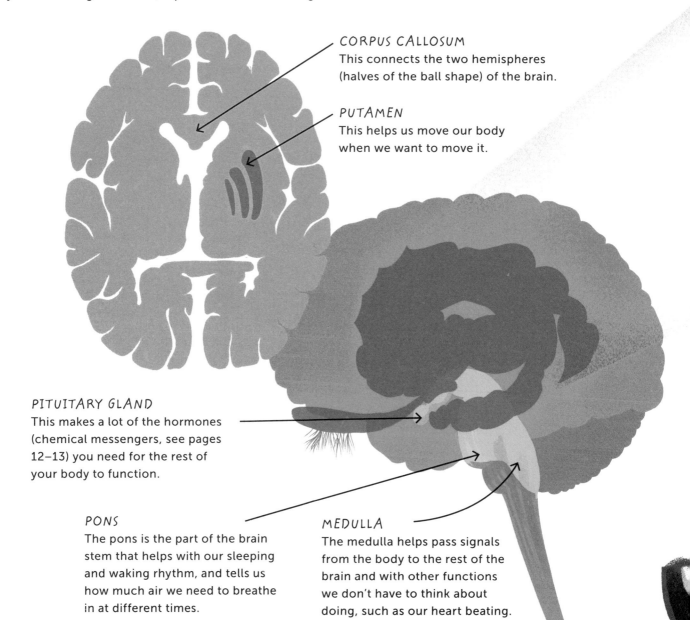

CORPUS CALLOSUM
This connects the two hemispheres (halves of the ball shape) of the brain.

PUTAMEN
This helps us move our body when we want to move it.

PITUITARY GLAND
This makes a lot of the hormones (chemical messengers, see pages 12–13) you need for the rest of your body to function.

PONS
The pons is the part of the brain stem that helps with our sleeping and waking rhythm, and tells us how much air we need to breathe in at different times.

MEDULLA
The medulla helps pass signals from the body to the rest of the brain and with other functions we don't have to think about doing, such as our heart beating.

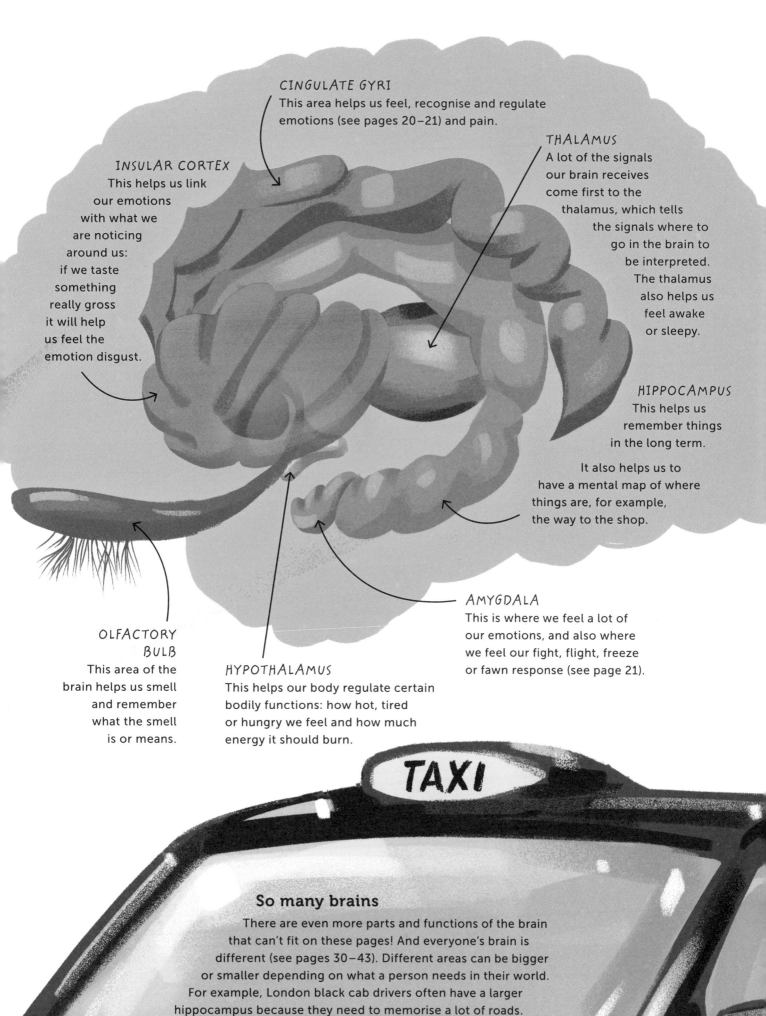

CINGULATE GYRI
This area helps us feel, recognise and regulate emotions (see pages 20–21) and pain.

THALAMUS
A lot of the signals our brain receives come first to the thalamus, which tells the signals where to go in the brain to be interpreted. The thalamus also helps us feel awake or sleepy.

INSULAR CORTEX
This helps us link our emotions with what we are noticing around us: if we taste something really gross it will help us feel the emotion disgust.

HIPPOCAMPUS
This helps us remember things in the long term.

It also helps us to have a mental map of where things are, for example, the way to the shop.

OLFACTORY BULB
This area of the brain helps us smell and remember what the smell is or means.

HYPOTHALAMUS
This helps our body regulate certain bodily functions: how hot, tired or hungry we feel and how much energy it should burn.

AMYGDALA
This is where we feel a lot of our emotions, and also where we feel our fight, flight, freeze or fawn response (see page 21).

TAXI

So many brains
There are even more parts and functions of the brain that can't fit on these pages! And everyone's brain is different (see pages 30–43). Different areas can be bigger or smaller depending on what a person needs in their world. For example, London black cab drivers often have a larger hippocampus because they need to memorise a lot of roads.

If our mind is related to our thoughts, *how* do we think? You've probably heard people talk about brain waves – let's have a look at how those 'waves' work.

HOW THE BRAIN MAKES THE MIND THINK

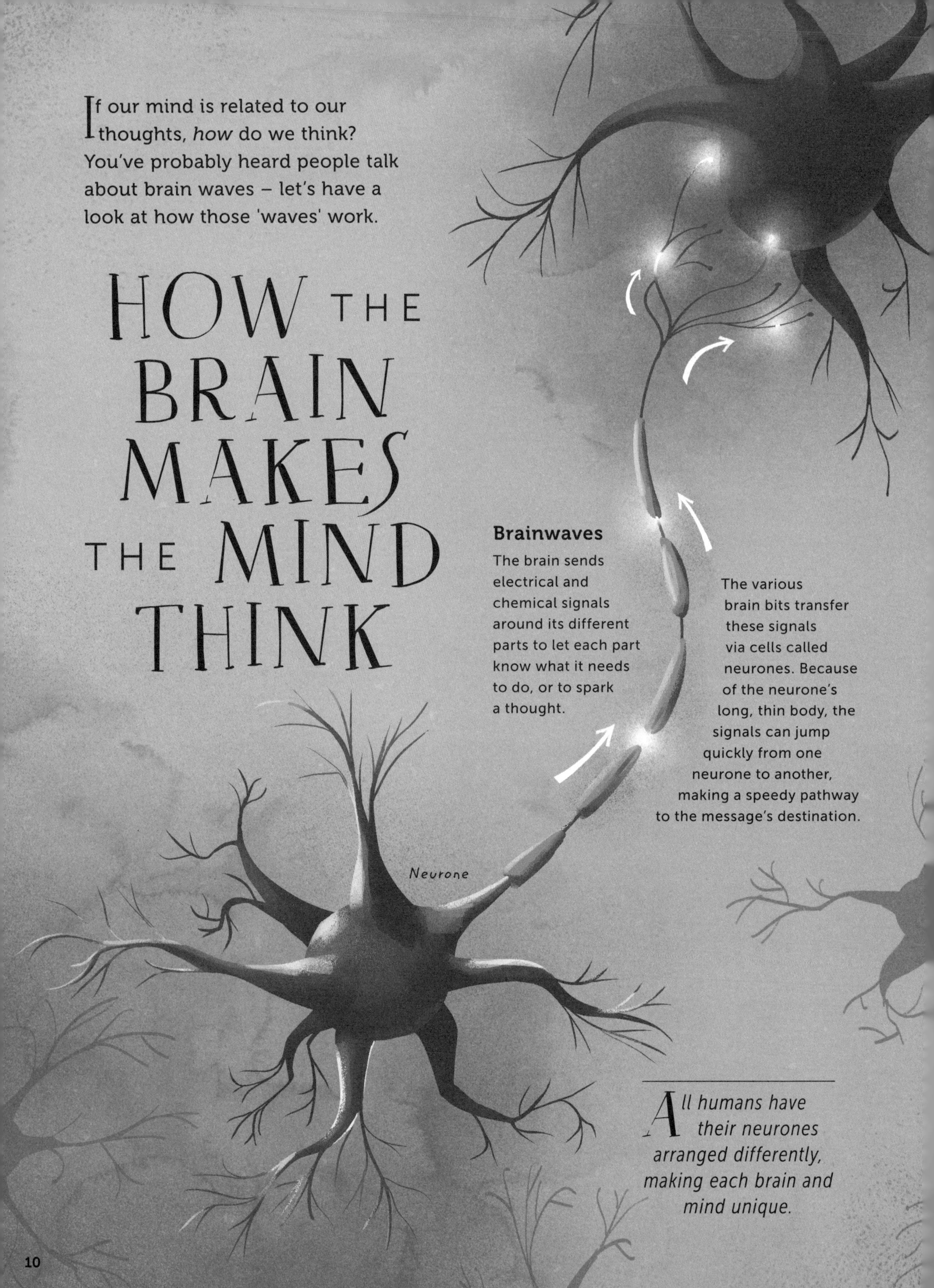

Brainwaves

The brain sends electrical and chemical signals around its different parts to let each part know what it needs to do, or to spark a thought.

The various brain bits transfer these signals via cells called neurones. Because of the neurone's long, thin body, the signals can jump quickly from one neurone to another, making a speedy pathway to the message's destination.

Neurone

All humans have their neurones arranged differently, making each brain and mind unique.

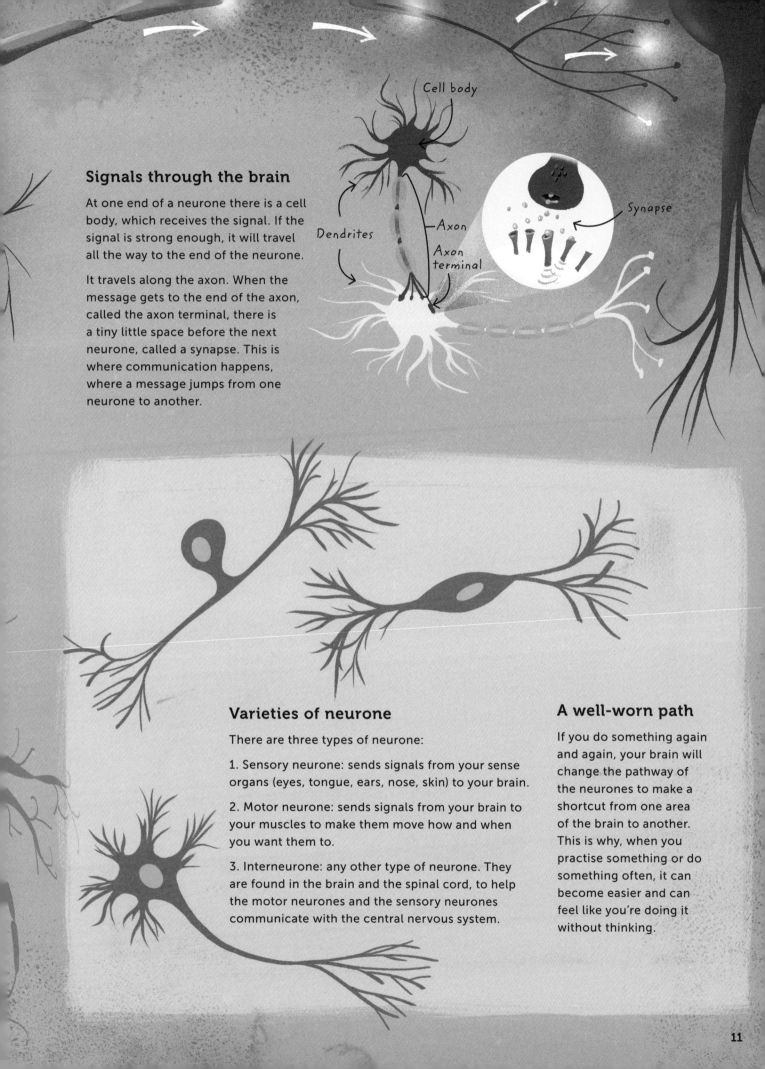

Signals through the brain

At one end of a neurone there is a cell body, which receives the signal. If the signal is strong enough, it will travel all the way to the end of the neurone.

It travels along the axon. When the message gets to the end of the axon, called the axon terminal, there is a tiny little space before the next neurone, called a synapse. This is where communication happens, where a message jumps from one neurone to another.

Cell body

Dendrites

Axon

Axon terminal

Synapse

Varieties of neurone

There are three types of neurone:

1. Sensory neurone: sends signals from your sense organs (eyes, tongue, ears, nose, skin) to your brain.

2. Motor neurone: sends signals from your brain to your muscles to make them move how and when you want them to.

3. Interneurone: any other type of neurone. They are found in the brain and the spinal cord, to help the motor neurones and the sensory neurones communicate with the central nervous system.

A well-worn path

If you do something again and again, your brain will change the pathway of the neurones to make a shortcut from one area of the brain to another. This is why, when you practise something or do something often, it can become easier and can feel like you're doing it without thinking.

CHEMICAL MESSAGES

Your brain and mind have a unique way of sending messages back and forth. They do it through special chemicals called neurotransmitters and hormones. These help our mind understand the incredible stories our brain wants to tell us!

Cell body

Neurotransmitter

Receptor

Synapse

What are neurotransmitters?

Neurotransmitters are different chemicals the brain makes and uses to send signals around the body via neurones (see pages 10–11). Their purpose is to help neurones to communicate with each other. Different types of neurotransmitter help in different ways.

Some tell your brain to *remember* something, some tell the brain to *stop doing* something, and others simply tell your brain that a system in your body might need *tweaking*.

Even though the word neurotransmitter has *neuro* – meaning brain – in it, we have neurotransmitters all around our body. For example, 95 per cent of the body's serotonin (a neurotransmitter that helps us regulate our mood, sleep and appetite) is found in the *bowel* not in the brain.

This can also be why you feel emotions all around your body, not just your brain. Have you ever felt butterflies in your stomach? Neurotransmitters in your gut is why!

What are hormones?

Hormones are another type of chemical that carries messages around the body. Hormones travel in the bloodstream to give instructions and tell different parts of the body to do things. For example, the hormone insulin tells your cells that they need to take in sugar so they have energy.

What's the difference?

Neurotransmitters and hormones have a very similar role and it can get even more confusing because some neurotransmitters are hormones too! An easy way to remember the difference is that **neurotransmitters** help **neurones** to communicate with each other, whereas **hormones** have specific instructions and tell a particular **part of the body** what to do.

OTHER ANIMALS AND THE MIND

Are humans the only animals that have unique and complex minds? How can we *know* if an animal has a mind or just instincts? Below are some features that psychologists and philosophers think make up a mind, which show up in many non-human species.

1: Communication

As humans, we communicate in so many ways: talking, using sign language and through writing, facial expressions and body language.

In the animal world, different animals communicate in a variety of ways, too.

• Bats use sounds, such **as** chirps and screeches, to communicate.

• The electric eel communicates using electrical pulses.

• Ants use chemicals called pheromones to tell other ants where good food is.

• Forager honey bees wiggle their bum – called a waggle dance – to tell other bees where to find good pollen.

2: Curiosity

Curiosity is about wanting to know something. In humans, curiosity has helped shape science, technology, engineering, philosophy, psychology, art and music among many other things.

Lots of animals, such as parrots, cats, elephants and octopuses, love to explore their surroundings and will actively try to learn new things. A curious animal understands that it can learn something new.

3: Play

The purpose of play is to have fun, but it also helps us learn about the rules and boundaries of our environment. Sometimes when your cat knocks something over, they're playing with their environment to learn how things work. This is called **locomotive play**.

Another type of play is called **social play**. Researchers have found dolphins playing catch or chase with each other. Play helps dolphins learn and practise social and communication skills, such as teamwork and using their voice.

4: Problem-solving

Crows are known for their problem-solving skills. One way they do this is by making tools from found objects to get at insects in small crevices. They have also been seen dropping hard-shelled nuts onto roads, waiting for cars to crack them open and expose the food inside.

Crows' ability to form strategies to get food shows researchers that these birds have minds capable of complex thought.

5: Personalities

Just like people, animals often have a unique personality. Some dogs might be super playful and friendly, while others are more reserved and shy. This means that dogs have thoughts, feelings and preferences and can make choices.

6: Specialised skills

Archer fish are amazing creatures that have a unique skill – they can spit a stream of water in just the right way to knock insects off leaves and branches so that they can eat them. This requires a lot of skill and coordination, which shows that they can think and problem-solve.

Researchers have found that archer fish are also able to learn and adapt their spitting techniques to different situations.

THE CHANGING BRAIN

How do our brains make sure they're the best brains for us? How do they change to adapt to our environment?

Baby brain power

The people whose brains (and minds!) change the most are babies. Because we don't know where in the world we're going to be born, or what family we're going to be born into, we have to be born with brains that can adapt.

For example, if grown-ups are shown pictures of two different friends, most can tell them apart by just looking at their faces.

But would they be able to do this for monkeys? Or meerkats? Scientists have done experiments showing that human babies can tell if you're showing them a picture of the same or a different monkey. Babies can also recognise different types of speech sounds that their parents cannot.

A baby's brain can have over 100 billion neurones (communication pathways in the brain), whereas an adult typically has only 86 billion.

Changing as we grow

Our brains are super flexible. To help you adapt to your environment, your brain's neurone connections are like a big puzzle that can rearrange its pieces whenever it wants. This is called neuroplasticity, and it helps our minds become more advanced and learn about the world. This means we may lose skills we don't need, such as being able to tell the difference between different monkeys' faces.

The brain in old age

There are lots of changes that happen in the brain as we age. One of these is that the brain doesn't make as many neurones, which can affect how quickly it can adapt to new situations.

Another change is that the brain doesn't make as many neurotransmitters (see pages 12–13), which can be important for learning and memory. This doesn't mean learning and remembering is impossible, it just means that it might take a little longer.

THE CHANGING MIND

Have you ever changed your mind about something? Maybe you didn't like a certain food when you were younger, but now you love it? Our changing brain means we can change how we think, feel or what we believe about something, too!

Believing in change

Have you ever heard the saying, "You can't teach an old dog new tricks"? Well, the good news is, thanks to neuroplasticity (see page 17), this isn't true.

Truly believing in the potential of your mind to change can have an impact on your actions and mindsets.

Growth mindset

A scientist and psychologist called Carol Dweck came up with the term 'growth mindset' in the early 2000s.

To have a growth mindset means you believe your brain and mind can always change and learn new things. It means you know you can overcome failures and, given enough time and support, you can learn anything you want and develop into who you want to be.

Firing up change

When we change our mind about a decision we've previously made, loads of neurones all over our brain start firing off chemical signals. It's almost like our brain is having a chemical discussion, to get everything up-to-date. These changes happen mostly in the pre-frontal cortex (see page 7) and in another part of the brain responsible for eye movements, called the eye field.

Our own mind

When you go to a birthday party, you'll notice that there are those who love loud music or the crack of a balloon popping, and those who don't. Likes and dislikes like this are all part of what we call our temperament, which is our unique personality 'fingerprint', or how different people react to different situations and emotions.

But these traits aren't fixed, either! Our temperament can change throughout our lives, thanks to growth mindset and neuroplasticity.

Unleash your brain's power

Growth mindset is a skill you can practise and improve! This can be done by staying physically active, eating healthy foods, being with friends, doing a puzzle, playing a game, trying a new instrument or learning a new language.

Try for yourself!

Why don't you pick one of the following things to give your brain a workout:

- Write with the other hand.

- Walk a different way home.

- Swap or put up new drawings on the wall.

- Try a new food.

EMOTIONS IN THE BRAIN

Humans are often described as emotional beings. Our emotions help us manage our understanding of the world and often influence our actions. Understanding the emotions we're feeling is very closely linked to the languages we speak and where we grow up, both of which affect our brains.

Two ways of understanding emotions

Top-down

One way researchers think we feel emotions is called **top-down**. This means that we look at the world around us and process in our brain what is happening. Then we're able to label the emotion and feel it in our body.

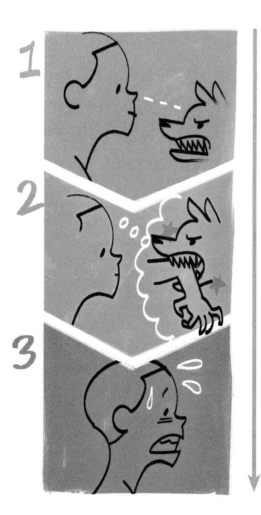

Bottom-up

Another way some researchers think we feel emotions is called **bottom-up**. This means that when something happens in your world, you feel an emotion in your body and then you think about what to label it with your brain.

What does this mean?

It doesn't really matter if you think you feel your emotions top-down one day and bottom-up the next. If we feel emotions in our body either way, what role does the brain have in these emotions, compared to the mind (see pages 22–23)?

How does the brain feel emotions?

There are lots of different areas in the brain that help us feel emotions. One of the main areas is the amygdala (see page 9), which also helps us link our emotions with memories. This is a two-way process.

Sometimes, when you remember a memory, it will change the emotion you're feeling in the present. Like when you remember your favourite trip or birthday present and it cheers you up in the moment.

But sometimes, if you remember something when you're already sad, you can change the memory itself to be a sad one.

It's not the amygdala alone that processes emotions. Even the experts can't tell you exactly where it all happens in the brain – every person feels each emotion slightly differently and through different avenues of the brain.

Fight, flight, freeze or fawn

When something scary or surprising happens to us, we can sometimes react without even thinking. This is what's called our fight, flight, freeze or fawn response.

FIGHT: we are ready to take on what's in front of us and may have an angry or physical reaction.

FLIGHT: we want to leave the situation and go to a safer place.

FREEZE: we remain unmoving and often silent.

FAWN: we try to please others or avoid arguments.

All of these responses are natural and automatic – to keep us safe and to react quickly to an immediate danger.

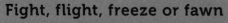

EMOTIONS IN THE MIND

*S*o, how do emotions affect us as people with unique minds? What do these brain processes mean for our everyday, real-life experiences?

Dealing with big emotions

When we face an emotion, our complex minds can sometimes have quite a complex reaction! We might process the emotional information based on what's happening *right now*, or what we think *might* happen, or memories of what *has happened before*, or by watching what has happened to *other people*. Or sometimes many of these, all at once!

This can all feel very complicated and can lead to big emotions that feel hard to deal with. In this case, we might need help to get our minds and bodies in a place where we can deal with tricky emotions as we feel them. This is called emotion regulation.

*S*ometimes our emotions can be so big that it's all we can think about. It's important that we feel our emotions – they are our brain's way of telling us how we should react to something.

Emotional regulation practices

- **Asking for help**

This might mean talking to a trusted adult or friend about what you're feeling or having a hug.

- **Being in nature**

Some people find nature helps them feel calmer. Depending on where you live, you could walk in the woods, park or beach. Some find caring for a plant at home helps in this same way.

- **Focus on breathing**

Taking some deep breaths – in for a few seconds, out for a few seconds – can help some people feel calmer and focused on the present moment.

- **Doing a favourite activity**

Some people have an activity that always makes them feel clearer about what they're feeling. This can be drawing, walking outside, tidying – whatever it is, taking a few moments can help manage big emotions.

- **Moving your body**

For some, moving their body helps them think through their feelings and feel more in control. This might be running, dancing, yoga, tai chi or something like stimming (repeating a movement or vocalisation).

- **Listening to music**

Some like to listen to music that matches their emotions – sad music when they're sad or happy music when they're happy. Others like 'calming music' or sounds from nature for whatever emotion they're feeling.

- **Meditation**

There is a popular type of meditation called mindfulness, which is about focusing on your body and what you're feeling in the present moment. You can practise mindfulness sitting, lying down or standing.

Other people like to meditate whilst walking or slowly moving their body through yoga or tai chi poses.

HOW DOES REMEMBERING WORK?

Our brain is constantly taking in information from what we see, hear, smell or taste. It has to decide what it's going to remember and what it's not. Memories are formed in lots of different parts of the brain, all working together. Let's take a look at some of them.

Visual memory

The hippocampus (see page 9) is like a special camera in your brain. When you experience something new, such as your first day of school or a fun trip, the hippocampus takes a snapshot of the memory so you can look back on it later.

Organising memories

The cerebral cortex (see page 6) is like a big filing cabinet where your long-term memories are kept. Each memory is like a file. The hippocampus helps to organise these files, and the cerebral cortex sorts them into categories, such as "fun times with friends" or "learning new things at school".

The feeling of memories

The amygdala is like your brain's emotion sensor. It adds feelings to your memories. When something makes you happy, excited, scared or even sad, the amygdala takes note. This sometimes make emotional memories very vivid, and stick out strongly in your mind.

Remembering the motions

The cerebellum (see page 6) is like your brain's skill centre. It is all about helping you remember how to do things, such as riding a bike, tying your shoelaces or playing a musical instrument. It helps with more physical memory, or what some people call muscle memory – when your body remembers how to do something without you feeling like you need to think too hard about it.

Scientists haven't yet found a limit to our memory – meaning we can remember more things than the internet can store! Test your memory – see the challenges on page 46.

TYPES OF LONG-TERM MEMORY

There are lots of different types of long-term memory. Let's explore the different types and how they come into use each day by following Sam's morning routine.

Sam's Many Memories: a story

When we have a memory of a sound, it's called **echoic memory**.

When we have a memory of what something feels like, it's called **haptic memory**.

When we remember or learn a fact – it's called **semantic memory**.

Memories about ourselves are called **autobiographical memory**. In this example, Sam is actually showing two types of autobiographical memory.

When we say a fact about ourselves – how old we are, for example – this is called **semantic autobiographical memory**. These memories are not linked to a time, place or event.

When we remember events from our past – such as a drink shooting out our nose – we are using our **episodic autobiographical memory**. We can relive an event about ourselves that happened in the past.

When we try to remember to do something in the future, this is called **prospective memory**.

Memory for doing activities that you don't even have to think about is called **procedural memory**. Examples of this can be physical, such as riding your bike or brushing your teeth, or they can be mental, such as remembering how to solve a puzzle. You don't have to try very hard to remember how to do it, your mind just knows.

Why Do We Sleep?

Most people, once per day, lie down, close their eyes and stay in the same place for several hours. We call this sleep – but why do we do it? And what does it have to do with our minds?

The sleep cycle

This whole cycle lasts about 90 minutes. We need to go through it several times in order to feel rested after a night's sleep.

1. First stage of sleep

We're dozy and tired, somewhere between awake and asleep. Our eyes and body are restful.

2. Second stage of sleep

Our eyes and body are still restful, but our body temperature drops. This is why it's often difficult to get to sleep when it's really hot outside – it's difficult for our body to drop to the temperature it needs to fall asleep.

4. Fourth stage of sleep:

Our body is restful but our brain and eyes are very active. Because our eyes are so active, this stage is called Rapid Eye Movement (REM) sleep. This when we dream.

3. Third stage of sleep:

Our muscles relax, our heart rate drops and our breathing slows. This is the stage of sleep many people call 'deep sleep'. It can be hard to wake someone up in this stage. This is also when someone is most likely to sleepwalk.

Your brain doesn't sleep

Whilst it may seem like you're not doing much when you're asleep, your brain is very active, doing lots of important things.

It makes pathways for neurotransmitters based on what you did that day. Your brain makes new, or strengthens existing, pathways to make things easier for next time. If you don't use the information or skill again, your brain will eventually change the pathways to things you do more often.

Your brain also gets rid of waste chemicals whilst you're asleep. Just like how your body needs to get rid of waste (by going to the toilet).

Sleep is important for our physical health, too, as our body only grows when we're asleep.

Our bodies naturally want to feel sleepy when it's dark and alert when it's light. This is called a circadian rhythm.

Why do we dream?

Did you know everyone dreams every single night? Scientists think that we dream three to six different dreams a night but that we forget about 95 per cent of the dreams we have.

And people dream differently! Do you dream in colour or black and white? Do you dream in photos or are your dreams like a film? Are you watching the film or starring in it?

Scientists think we dream in order to help organise our thoughts and emotions. This is why, if you're feeling particularly worried, it might come up in your dream. Or if you're facing a creative problem, you might come up with the answer in a dream.

MANY MARVELLOUS MINDS

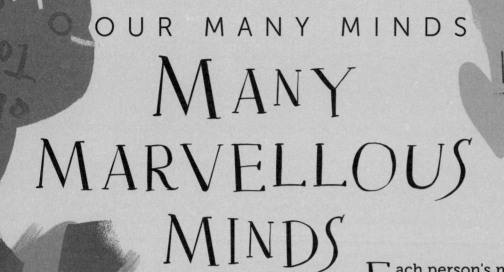

Each person's mind is unique to them. Everyone has different experiences and has a different personality. There's no one way that a brain should be structured – the variety of brains and minds is a natural part of human life.

The wonderful wide world of nature

In nature, one plant might attract pollinators with its bright, bold colours, while another attracts pollinators with its strong smell or misleading shape. Neither of these plants are better than the other – just different. This is called biodiversity in the natural world, and when we talk about different brains, we call it neurodiversity.

Neurodiversity

Neurodiversity is a word to describe the fact that everyone thinks, feels, learns and processes the world differently. And this is something to celebrate. These differences are what makes humanity so extraordinary, as everyone has different strengths and viewpoints.

Neurotypical is a word used to describe people who think, feel and process the world in a way that fits in with the cultural 'norm'. A person who thinks, feels and processes the world differently to this may be considered 'neurodivergent' – diverting or different from the 'norm'.

Some in the second category may feel their environment doesn't support how they think, feel, learn and process the world. This may mean that they ask for support or adjustments to navigate the world, or to feel accepted for who they are.

Neurodivergent names

Some people seek out a label, called a diagnosis, for their neurodivergence. This may help them to feel part of a wider group or community or help them to ask for support from others. Some diagnoses that fall under the neurodivergent umbrella include:

- Attention Deficit Hyperactivity Disorder (ADHD)
- Autism
- Developmental Language Disorder (DLD)
- Dyscalculia
- Dyslexia
- Dyspraxia/Developmental Co-ordination Disorder (DCD)
- Epilepsy
- Foetal Alcohol Spectrum Disorder (FASD)
- Intellectual Disability
- Pathological Demand Avoidance (PDA)
- Specific Learning Disorders/Differences
- Stammer
- Tourette's Syndrome
- Tic Disorders

Turn to page 47 for a full definition of each, as adapted from the definition of each diagnoses by the *DSM-5*, American Psychiatric Association (2013).

EXPLORING THE WORLD OF NEURODIVERSITY

Imagine if all humans had the exact same job. That would be quite boring. The world is such a fascinating place because we have dancers and engineers, farmers and doctors. Everyone has different interests, skills and needs, and different minds to go with them.
This is neurodiversity!

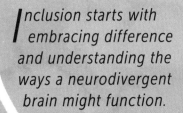

Inclusion starts with embracing difference and understanding the ways a neurodivergent brain might function.

Embracing neurodiversity

Our world has always been neurodiverse, but we've not always used this word to describe it. Today, as we understand more about the brain and our unique minds, we know it's important for schools, workplaces and wider society to understand neurodiversity.
This means building a more inclusive world where everyone feels supported to be who they are and to live the life they wish to live.

Deep focus: understanding monotropism

Have you ever been so focused on one thing that you didn't realise what was going on around you? For example, you were playing a video game and you didn't hear your dad tell you that dinner's ready?

For some people, when their brain finds a 'hook', they naturally turn all their attention towards it and they are able to block everything else out. This means they can focus on an activity for a long period of time, which is called a monotropic state.

This allows them to explore something deeply, or complete a complex task, often without realising how much time has passed. This is called monotropism.

People in a monotropic state can sometimes find it difficult to stop or switch task. This means they may not hear you or may get overwhelmed if they need to change task quickly. It's important to know that this isn't deliberate – their brain has blocked everything else out to allow them to focus on one thing.

Multi-focus: understanding polytropism

Have you ever enjoyed listening to music whilst having a conversation? Or kept a podcast on while doing schoolwork?

Some people's minds thrive on having lots of stimulation at the same time. This means that if they are in a situation where there's lots of different bits of information coming at them, they can process all the details at once without getting overwhelmed. This is called polytropism.

Monotropism and polytropism

Some neurodivergent people find their brain naturally leans more towards monotropism whereas others' brains lean more towards polytropism. Most people will experience both monotropism and polytropism in their life, but they are more common for neurodivergent people. These two different ways of processing information have strengths for different situations.

CAN HUMANS READ MINDS?

Have you ever seen clips of 'mind-readers' who seem to know what people are thinking and feeling without asking them? Do these magicians truly have mind-reading powers? Or are they using clues to do some clever guessing? Scientists and researchers explore these questions as they consider the 'theory of mind'.

How we 'read' minds

Theory of mind is an idea that explores how someone can grasp other people's thoughts, feelings, beliefs and behaviours without them directly saying what they are.

It is not something that we're born being able to do, but through our social interactions, and as our minds develop, we're able to understand more about how other people think. As we gather experiences in life, we can all begin to read others' thoughts to some extent!

Stages of understanding

There are different theories of mind that develop at different stages of life.

Stage 1: from a young age, children start to develop the ability to see that other people have their own beliefs, desires and goals.

Stage 2: after this, we learn that people can believe untrue facts or have 'false beliefs'.

Stage 3: next, we learn that people's unique minds have an impact on their actions. At this stage, we also begin to learn how to see the world from someone else's point of view.

Stage 4: as we learn and develop, we begin to understand that people can have beliefs about *other people's* beliefs, desires, emotions and goals.

Stage 5: then, as we grow up and experience different social situations, we start to decode facial expressions and body language.

Adults still learn and develop these skills and their theory of mind throughout their life as they experience new things.

The discovery of lying

When we start to understand that people can have different thoughts, feelings and beliefs to us, we also start to learn how to lie. We realise that we can fill in the gaps of what someone doesn't know and get them to believe something that isn't true.

Have you ever told a lie? Even a teeny tiny one? As much as parents hate it, children learning to lie is an important developmental stage. It's part of your theory of mind! If you decide to lie, it means you are beginning to understand Stage 1 and Stage 2 (see above). To lie, you also need to understand that beliefs can be changed or tricked (part of Stage 3).

However, the *reasons* you might lie can be a lot more complex. These are often linked to the emotions we're feeling and the culture we live in.

WHAT IS MENTAL HEALTH?

Everyone has mental health. Mental health just means how our mind is feeling and if we are well enough to deal with certain stresses, achieve our goals, learn at school and do the things we enjoy.

A wide spectrum

There are many layers and varieties of mental unwellness, just as there are different types of physical unwellness.

Sometimes we get a little cut and we can help our bodies get better by ourselves or with the help of family and friends. This kind of hurt doesn't stop us from living our day-to-day life.

Sometimes we might have a flu for a few days, but with some rest and medicine our bodies feel better. And sometimes people have a physical illness that they live with and must treat every day.

Whatever the illness is, you don't choose how and when you become physically ill. The same is true for your mental health. And just as there are many people to help you if you become physically ill, there are many people to help you if your mind feels unwell.

Having some kind of physical illness at some point is very common, and the same is true for mental health. Two common issues relating to mental health are explained on the next page.

Generalised Anxiety Disorder

This is usually when someone feels so much worry that it has an impact on their thoughts and can stop them from living the life they want to.

Some people with generalised anxiety disorder feel on-edge and restless day and night. Others feel really tired all the time because constantly feeling anxious can be exhausting for the mind and body.

Major Depressive Disorder

This is usually when someone doesn't feel any joy. Often people with depression say they feel numb and even doing their favourite things can feel like a chore.

Some people with major depressive disorder feel tired all the time and can't stay awake, whereas others find it difficult to sleep. Some people want to eat all the time, and others don't want to eat at all.

Everyday mental health

To help keep our minds healthy, our bodies have natural and regular reactions of either fight, flight, freeze or fawn mode (see page 21) to help us deal with a stressful situation.

There are lots of other symptoms that go along with any mental health diagnosis. So, if you are concerned about yourself or someone else, please talk to a trusted adult.

KEEPING OUR MINDS HEALTHY

We don't choose whether our bodies and minds get sick, but there are some things that we can do to help us try to stay healthy and feel the best we possibly can (although these things don't mean we won't ever get sick!).

Exercise

Our mind and our body are connected. We often feel better just by moving and breathing, such as in the practices of yoga and tai chi. These can help us regulate and express our emotions (see pages 22–23).

When our bodies get fully warmed up and sweaty, our brain releases chemicals called endorphins. Endorphins have lots of benefits for the body, including helping us feel less stressed, feel less pain, feel happier and helping our brain get rid of waste chemicals quicker.

Healthy eating

Eating a healthy and balanced diet not only keeps your body fit and strong, but also helps keep your brain working as it should. A lot of the vitamins and minerals found in healthy foods – such as leafy greens, legumes, lentils, beans and fish – help our brain to think, grow and work. These foods also help the brain to change and create neurones (see pages 10–11).

Sleep

Getting good-quality sleep is important for mental health because the brain is busy sorting and organising itself as you sleep, as well as getting rid of any waste (see pages 28–29).

On top of that, we feel grumpy, tired and probably more stressed without good sleep.

Here are some top tips to get a good night's sleep:

- Spend some time before bedtime relaxing, doing a calming activity.

- Don't have lights that are too bright in line with your eyes where you sleep.

- Reduce disruptive noises (some people like silence and some block disruptions using nature sounds or white noise).

Mindfulness and meditation

Practising mindfulness and meditation can help regulate our emotions (see pages 22–23), and have been shown to increase the size of the pre-frontal cortex in the brain, which helps with decision-making, concentration and future-planning. It can also help us cope better with pain and build connections with others (such as being kinder, more compassionate and more accepting).

Babies are born with more neurones than adults. Their brain then 'prunes' these neurones according to their experiences – so how do brains differ around the world, in different cultures?

CULTURAL PERSPECTIVES

Two main cultures

Some researchers split the world into two main cultural types. These are 'independent' cultures and 'interdependent' cultures. Of course not all cultures fit into these two groups, but most people can recognise some aspects of each group wherever they live in the world.

Independent cultures are made up of people who tend to care about being unique and self-sufficient.

Interdependent cultures care more about fitting in and being equal.

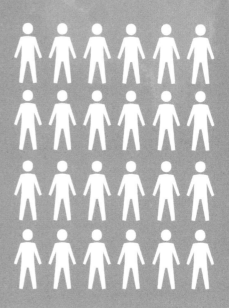

Same picture, different minds

Scientists have found that if you're from an independent culture, you tend to focus on the main object of a picture, and for longer. This means that if someone changed something in that front object, you'd be more likely to spot it.

If you're from an interdependent culture, you tend to focus on what is happening in the whole of a picture. This means that if someone changed something in the background of a picture, you'd be more likely to spot the change.

Same fish, different minds

When shown an image like the one below, with a school of fish swimming in one direction, if you're from an independent culture you're more likely to think that the front fish is swimming in that direction because it wants to, whereas if you're from an interdependent culture you're more likely to think the front fish is swimming that way because the group is.

Test yourself!

Have a look at the two horizontal lines below.
Are they the same size or are they two different sizes?

If you see the lines as different lengths you may be from a more independent culture.

If you see the lines as the same length you may be from a more interdependent culture.

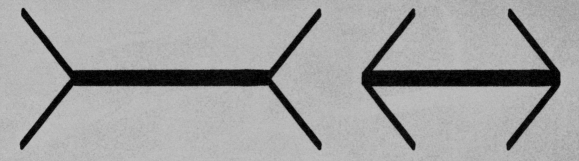

Researchers don't know why this is — can you think of any reason our minds might see these differently?

The is based on the experiment designed by Franz Carl Müller-Lyer.

HOW DOES LANGUAGE AFFECT OUR MIND?

Language is a massive part of how we think, communicate and interact with the world around us. But there are over 7,000 languages all around the world! How does the language we speak affect the way our minds understand the world around us?

Colours and languages around the world

Did you know that the language you speak can affect what colours you see?
Test yourself and see how easily you can spot the odd one out.

If you would name these colours using two different words, then you may be a Russian speaker. People whose languages would name them as the same colour find it harder to see the odd one out.

If there's one shape here that you would call a different colour, then you may be an Otjihimba speaker. Those whose languages would name them all the same colour would find it harder to see the odd one out.

If there's one shape here that you would call a different colour, then you may be an English speaker. Those whose languages would name them all the same colour would find it harder to see the odd one out.

Time-travelling language

If you have to move a party from 2 pm to 10 am are you pushing it back or bringing it forward? Not everyone agrees on this around the world!

How your language talks about time can affect how your mind thinks you're travelling through time. This can also affect whether you think you're moving through your life looking into the future, looking into the past, or if the past, present and future are circular. Some cultures view the past as done and unchanging and the future as something that they can actively change. However, in other cultures, they view the past, present and future as interconnected and all affecting one another.

Emotions and languages around the world

There are so many words across all the different languages to describe how we're feeling. Some languages have lots of emotion words and others only have a few. Some languages have multiple words to describe similar emotions and others have very clear differences among a smaller set of emotions.

This can affect what emotions you think you're feeling, and how you express them. In some cultures with lots of emotion words, people are very happy to talk about emotions, whereas in other cultures it can be seen as rude or too blunt.

CELEBRATING THE HUMAN MIND

Throughout this book we have learned many details about how the brain and mind can do some amazing things! Does this mean that scientists know everything about what's going on in our heads? Absolutely not!

So many scientists

There are lots of different areas of research that help us learn more about the mind.

There are **psychologists** (who focus on behaviour and the mind), **neuroscientists** (who focus on the brain and biology), **sociologists** (who focus on society) and **anthropologists** (who focus on culture and what we can learn from historic cultures).

By coming together with their knowledge and skills, experts can develop new treatments for disorders, as well as increase our understanding of human behaviours and thoughts. The goal is to unlock the secrets of the mind and use this knowledge to improve the lives of people around the world.

What about *my* mind?

One of the main reasons it's hard for scientists and researchers to know everything about the brain and mind is because they're unique for everyone. There are more than 8 billion people on the planet and your brain is the perfect one just for you! It helps you live and survive in your life and makes you the expert of your own experiences.

Quick brain facts

- There are no nerve endings in your brain. If you have brain surgery, you're fully awake, as you won't feel a thing (once they numb the skull area of course)!

- We don't learn to smile by watching other people. Babies who are blind also smile when they're happy.

- Have you ever seen a face in your toast or in a tree's knots? That's because there's an area of the brain that is always looking for faces. It's called the fusiform face area.

- The brain uses 20 per cent of our body's energy even though it only makes up about two per cent of our body's weight.

- The brain can make enough electricity to power a small light bulb.

- The brain is able to process over 11 million pieces of information at the same time.

- Touching the brain organ feels very similar to touching tofu or jelly.

- If you laid out all the brain's blood vessels in long lines, they would stretch over 640 km.

- Your brain can imagine things that it has never seen or experienced before.

MIND GAMES

This activity is based on a real-life experiment that Harvard University scientists Daniel Simons and Christopher Chabris did called 'change blindness'.

Change blindness: your experiment

You will need:

- A group of people who know you
- A gathering or social event
- A change of clothes tucked away in a bag
- A small piece of paper and a pen (optional).

When you have a group of people around you, about halfway through your time together, go to the toilets and change your clothes. This doesn't have to be a complete change of clothes; it could be something like changing your T-shirt to one of a different colour.

Return to the group and wait to see if anyone notices or comments. If you want to, you could count the number of people who notice on a piece of paper, although you may be surprised how many people don't notice.

Change blindness: what's it about?

Change blindness is the term used in psychology for when people don't notice that something has changed. In the Harvard experiment, they asked people to watch a video of some people passing a basketball. Some people who watched the video didn't notice that one of the players changed their clothes halfway through.

This shows us that we often don't take in every tiny detail, but that some people notice details that others don't.

This activity explores how our working memory functions. You can read about this on pages 24–25.

Test your memory!

You will need:

- A pen
- Paper
- A window
- A table or something to lean on
- A friend or parent.

Find a window where you can comfortably see outside and draw. Draw something you can see outside while counting aloud backwards from 20.

Now ask your friend or parent to list five animals aloud. After they've said each animal, write the word on the other side of your paper, while counting backwards from 20 aloud.

How did you find this? Was one task harder than the other? What made one harder than the other, in your opinion?

If you can get some friends to try it, too, compare and contrast your experiences.

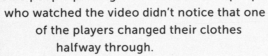

20 19 18 17 16 15 14 13 12 11 10 9 8 7 6

GLOSSARY

Attention Deficit Hyperactivity Disorder (ADHD) – a neurodivergent condition that affects attention span and controlling impulsive behaviours.

Autism – a neurodivergent condition that affects communication, social interaction and behaviour.

Axon – a long, thin part of a neurone that sends signals to other cells.

Axon terminal – the end of an axon that releases neurotransmitters to communicate with other neurones.

Bowel – the part of the digestive system that absorbs water from food waste and gets rid of it from the body as poo.

Broca's area – the area in your brain that helps you find the right words and turn your thoughts into speech.

Cells – the basic building blocks of life that make up all living things, including the human body.

Central nervous system – the system that goes from your brain and down your spine which helps you feel, think, breathe and move.

Consciousness – the state of being aware of your surroundings, thoughts, feelings and sensations.

Dendrite – a branch-like extension of a neurone that receives signals from other neurones.

Developmental Language Disorder (DLD) – a neurodivergent condition that affects understanding and using language to communicate.

Dyscalculia – a neurodivergent condition that affects maths skills and understanding and using numbers.

Dyslexia – a neurodivergent condition that affects reading and related language-based tasks.

Dyspraxia/Developmental Co-ordination Disorder (DCD) – a neurodivergent condition that affects fine motor skills and coordination.

Epilepsy – a neurodivergent condition where someone has recurring seizures (sudden and uncontrollable electrical signals firing in the brain) due to electrical disturbances in the brain.

Experiment – a scientific investigation to test a hypothesis and gather data.

Foetal Alcohol Spectrum Disorder – a group of neurodivergent conditions caused by alcohol consumption during pregnancy that can affect a person's physical and mental development.

Hormone – a chemical messenger produced by the body that regulates different functions of the body.

Hypothesis – a statement about what a researcher or scientist thinks they'll find by doing their experiment.

Intellectual Disability – a neurodivergent condition where someone may develop at a different rate to neurotypical people in skills such as academic learning, problem-solving and adapting to new situations.

Mindfulness – the practice of focusing on the present moment and paying attention to your thoughts, feelings and sensations without judgment.

Monotropism – a tendency to focus on only one thing or aspect of a situation.

Motor cortex – the area of the brain that tells your body how to move.

Nerve – a fibre in your body that sends electrical signals around your brain and from your brain to other parts of your body.

Neurone – a type of cell in the body's nervous system that transmits signals in the brain and throughout the body.

Neuroscientist – a scientist who studies the nervous system, including the brain and nerves.

Neurotransmitter – a chemical that transmits signals between neurones.

Optical illusion – the experience of seeing something that isn't there or that appears different than it is.

Pathological Demand Avoidance (PDA) – a neurodivergent condition (often present in those who are also autistic) that affects people's reactions to everyday demands and routines, such as following rules or completing tasks.

Philosopher – someone who studies and thinks about fundamental questions about existence, knowledge, values, reason, mind and language.

Polytropism – a tendency to focus on multiple things or multiple aspects of a situation.

Psychologist – someone who studies the mind and behaviour, and helps people with emotional and mental health problems.

Regulate – to maintain something within a desired level (not too high and not too low) so you can perform at your best.

Serotonin – a neurotransmitter that helps regulate mood, appetite and sleep.

Specific Learning Disorder/Differences – a neurodivergent condition that affects specific academic skills, such as reading, writing or maths.

Stammer – a neurodivergent condition that affects speaking fluency, with repeating or prolonging sounds or words.

Stimming – repeating a physical movement or vocalisation that people often do to regulate their emotions, such as to help them feel calm.

Theory – a scientific explanation for why things are the way they are, based on evidence and reasoning.

INDEX

adapting 16, 17
adults 22, 34, 35, 37, 40
animal world 14, 15
anthropologists 44

babies 14, 40
beliefs 4, 5, 18, 34, 35
bloodstream 13
brain 4–12, 16–22, 24–25, 28–30,
    32, 33, 38, 39, 44, 45
  amygdala 9, 21, 25
  brain stem 6
  cerebellum 6, 25
  cerebrum 6, 7
  cingulate gyri 9
  corpus callosum 8
  cross-section 8
  hemispheres 8
  hippocampus 9, 24
  hypothalamus 9
  insular cortex 9
  medulla 6, 8
  olfactory bulb 9
  pituitary gland 8
  pons 6, 8
  putamen 8
  thalamus 9
brainwaves 10

cells 10, 11, 13
central nervous system 11
Chabris, Christopher 46
changing your mind 18, 19
children 34, 35
circadian rhythm 29
communication 14–15, 16, 42
consciousness 4

cultures 40, 41, 43, 44
curiosity 14

delayed gratification 7
dreaming 28–29
Dweck, Carol 18

emotional regulation 22, 23, 38, 39
emotions (see also feelings) 9, 12,
    19, 20–23, 29, 34, 35, 38, 43
endorphins 38
energy 9, 13, 45
exercise 38
experiences 5, 24, 34, 40, 45

feelings (see also emotions) 4, 5,
    15, 18, 25, 34, 35
fight, flight, freeze or fawn
    response 9, 21, 37

Gopnik, Professor Alison 35
growth mindset 18, 19

healthy eating 38
hormones 8, 12, 13

imagination 4, 5, 45

languages 20, 42, 43
lies 35
long-term memory, types of 26, 27

memories 4–5, 7, 9, 21, 24–27, 46
mental health 36, 37, 39
mind 4, 5, 10, 12, 14–16, 18, 20, 22,
    30, 32–34, 37, 38, 40, 42–45
monotropism 33

neurodivergent 31–33
neurodiversity 30–32
neurones 10–13, 16, 17, 19, 38, 40
neuroplasticity 17–19
neuroscientists 5, 44
neurotransmitters 12, 13, 17, 29
neurotypical 31

pain 7, 9, 39
personalities 15, 30
philosophers 4, 5, 14
play 15
polytropism 33
problem-solving 15
psychologists 5, 14, 18, 44

researchers 5, 15, 20, 34, 40, 41, 45

scientists 4, 5, 18, 25, 29, 34, 39, 40,
    44, 46
senses 7, 9
Simons, Daniel 46
skull 4, 6, 7, 45
sleep 28–29, 37, 39
sociologists 44
spinal cord 11

temperament 19
theory of mind 34, 35
thoughts 4, 5, 7, 10, 15, 18, 29, 34,
    35, 37, 44

water 7, 15

FURTHER INFORMATION

MORE BOOKS TO READ

Adventures of the Brain
Written by Professor Sanjay Manohar and
illustrated by Gary Boller, Wayland 2024

The Kids' Guide series
Written by expert authors on a variety of
important topics and illustrated by Scott
Garrett, Franklin Watts 2022

WEBSITE AND CONTACTS IF YOU NEED SUPPORT

www.CAMHS-resources.co.uk
A website full of helpful resources for young people and
carers to help support mental health and well-being.

Childline (for Under 19s) 0800 1111 and www.childline.org.uk
For free, confidential advice whenever you need help.